KNIGHT
AGINCOURT

A ROLL OF HONOUR

By
Steve Archibald

REDCREST PUBLISHING

All Text and illustrations by Steve Archibald
unless otherwise noted

Copyright © 2019 Redcrest Publishing

ISBN: 978-1-9996677-3-3

Redcrest Publishing
9 Chalfont Close, Hemel Hempstead, Herts. HP2 7JR

Illustration information. Page 6 James E Doyle (1822-1892) (A Chronicle of England, Pg 367. Published by Longman, Green, Longman, Roberts & Green, 1864). Page 10, Edmund Blair Leighton (Cassell's History of England, Vol 1, Kings Ed. Pg 557, c.1906). Pages 8 & 9, Artist Unknown (British & Foreign Arms & Armour. Published by T C & E C Jack, 1909) and (Ancient Armour & Weapons in Europe Vol II. Published by John Henry & James Parker, 1860). Page 3, Unkown artist (Old England: A Pictorial Museum. Vol 1 published by C Knight & Co, 1845). Page 60, Henry J Ford (1860-1941) (A History of England. Published by Doubleday, Page & Co, 1911).

KNIGHTS OF AGINCOURT
A ROLL OF HONOUR

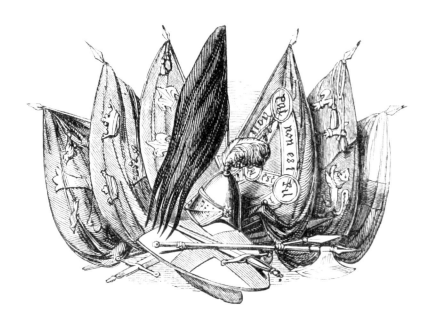

CONTENTS

INTRODUCTION

There have been a great many books written about the Battle of Agincourt, but none that I am aware of that tried to compile a pictorial armorial roll of both sides.

What I have included here is as many coat of arms of knights and other dignitaries that were actually at the battle. What I have found is only a fraction of numbers from both sides as information is rather thin on the ground.

On the English side I started with King Henry V's retinue list from the book 'History of the Battle of Agincourt' by Sir Harris Nicolas. It was a good starting point, however, not all the names included in this list actually made it to the Agincourt battlefield.

At the siege at Harfleur a large number of Henry's army fell foul to wounds or a serious outbreak of dysentery and died or were sent home. Also three dignitaries, the Earl of Cambridge, Sir Thomas Grey of Heton and Baron Scrope were executed for plotting against the king just before Henry set sail to France. Their individual retinues, however, do appear to have still continued on to France with Henry. One other factor that had to be taken into account was the men left behind at Harfleur to man the garrison. Estimates conclude that by the time Henry's army left Harfleur it had been reduced by as much as one third.

The main references used were ancestry web sites, L'Armorial General volumes I-V by J B Rietstap, Encyclopaedia of Heraldry or General Armory of England, Scotland and Ireland by John Burke 1851, www.historyofparliamentonline.org, plus many various armorial rolls of the time and many other books and web sites.

Information on participants for the French army is very scarce and I had to rely mostly on lists of those killed or taken prisoner for ransom.

For the French side I referenced ancestry web sites, L'Armorial General volumes I-V by J B Rietstap, 'Azincourt' by Rene de Belleval (excellent French language book) plus various armorial rolls of the time and many other books and web sites.

I hope that this book adds a little to details of this important point in history and will prove to be a handy reference for historians, artists and model makers, etc. S.A.

THE CAMPAIGN & BATTLE

The Battle of Agincourt was a major turning point during the Hundred Years War. England's victory against the numerically superior French army was totally unexpected. It crippled the French army and began a period of military success for the English.

King Henry's invasion of France came about when negotiations over his claim on Aquitaine and other French lands broke down. Early in 1415 a somewhat angry Henry started to collect funds and build an army. By August of that year the army set sail and landed in northern France. Henry immediately lay siege on the port of Harfleur to use as a base. The siege however took longer and was more costly than expected. The town surrendered on 22nd September but the English army had suffered many casualties through combat and disease.

With a depleted army and winter approaching Henry decided to march his army north to a friendly Calais to demonstrate his presence in the region rather than return straight home. On 8th October Henry left Harfleur leaving a small garrison in the town. By this time

During the height of the battle King Henry guards his injured younger brother the Duke of Gloucester from an attack by the Duke of Alencon. Sir Walter Hungerford rushes to defend his king.
(Illustration by James E Doyle)

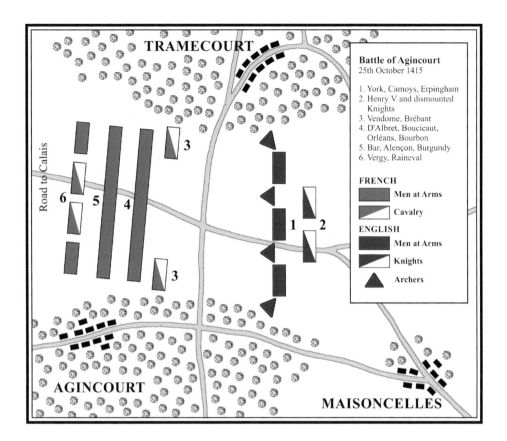

Battle of Agincourt
25th October 1415

1. York, Camoys, Erpingham
2. Henry V and dismounted Knights
3. Vendome, Brébant
4. D'Albret, Boucicaut, Orléans, Bourbon
5. Bar, Alençon, Burgundy
6. Vergy, Raineval

FRENCH
  Men at Arms
  Cavalry

ENGLISH
  Men at Arms
  Knights
  Archers

the French had assembled a sizeable army and headed towards cutting off the English armies' progress.

After shadowing the English army for a number of days the two armies moved to face each other on the 24th October. The French, however, declined to enter battle hoping for more troops to arrive. The following morning Henry moved his troops to engage the French, despite a long march having little or no food and suffering from disease.

The two armies lined up on a recently ploughed field between two wooded areas near the town of Agincourt (Azincourt). It had rained quite heavily the day before and would prove to be a significant factor in deciding the outcome. Descriptions of the

deployment of the two armies vary in detail from one source to another. Essentially Henry's men lined up between the woods in alternating formations of archers and men-at-arms. Henry in the center with the Duke of York and Lord Camoys commanding the left and right and Sir Erpingham marshalling the archers. Wooden stakes were installed in front the English line. Estimates for the total number of Englishmen is 6,000 to 9,000 of which one sixth were knights and men-at-arms and the rest longbowmen.

The French formed three wide formations of men-at-arms with some cavalry in the third and some archers and crossbowmen in the the second formation. These were commanded by the Dukes Alencon, Bar, Orleans and

Two typical examples of armour from the time of Agincourt taken from memorial brasses. Left, Sir Thomas Braunstone, 1401, Wisbeach Church, Cambridgeshire. Right, John Cray, Esquire, Chinnor, Oxfordshire. Circa 1390.

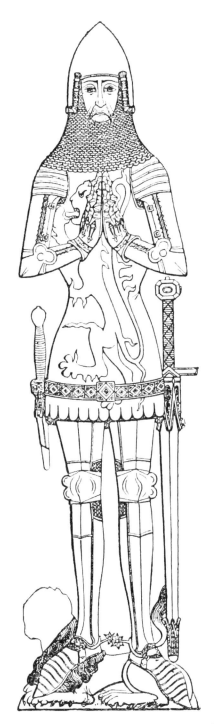

A further two typical examples of armour from the time of Agincourt taken from memorial brasses. Left, Sir George Felbrigge 1400, Playford Church, Suffolk. Right, Ralph Lord Stafford, from the Hastings Brass at Elsing, Norfolk.

The Thanksgiving Service on the field of Agincourt. (Illustration by Edmund Blair Leighton)

Bourbon and Auvergne; The Counts Nevers, Fauquembergues and Dammartin, plus Jean 'Boucicaut'Le Meingre.

Two large cavalry formations were at the front of these three lines to the left and right, commanded by the Count of Vendome and Admiral of France, Brébant. In command overall was Constable Charles d'Albret. In all French numbers estimate at around 12,000 to 36,000 knights and men-at-arms, plus unknown thousands of infantry, archers and crossbowmen.

From the outset French advances did not go well. The initial cavalry attack faltered as those that did reach the English line through a hail of arrows could not charge through the wooden stakes all the while being fired apon by longbowmen. The subsequent retreat churned up the muddy ground even

more, so that the men-at-arms had to travel through thick mud and around fallen comrades and horses wearing their heavy armour. Those that did reach the English line did initially push them back, but under a constant barrage of arrows from the longbow men followed by attack from much fresher English forces meant the exhausted French attack failed. When the French second line advanced they only added to the problem by pushing the first line into the English.

The fighting went on for about three hours until all the French commanders had been killed or taken prisoner. Seeing the battle lost many of the French not yet engaged left the battlefield without taking any part. Numbers of casualties vary but estimates range from just 100 to 450 for the English compared to the French 4,000 to 10,000.

ENGLISH COMBATANTS

THE COMMANDERS: PAGE 13

King Henry V	Thomas Lord Camoys
Edward Duke of York	Sir Thomas Erpingham

Humphrey, Duke of Gloucester

OTHER PERSONS OF DISTINCTION

PAGE 13
Sir William Argentine
Sir Richard Arundel
Sir John Assheton
Sir Roger Aston
Sir Thomas Babington
Sir Robert Babthorpe

PAGE 14
Sir John Baskerville
Sir John Beauchamp
Sir William Beauchamp
Sir Walter Beauchamp
Sir Charles Beaumont
John Bernard Esq
Sir John Blount
Sir Ralph Bostock
William Lord Botreaux
Sir William Bouchier
John de Burgh
Sir John Calfe

PAGE 15
Robert Castell Esq.
Sir Thomas Charles
Sir Thomas Chaworth
John Cheney Esq.
William Chesterton Esq.
Sir John Chichester
John Lord Clifford
William Lord Clinton
Sir Hertong von Clux

Sir John Codringham
Sir John Cole
Sir John Croker

PAGE 16
Sir John Colshill
Roger Corbet Esq.
Sir John Cornwall
Sir Edward Courtenay
Sir John Croker
Baron Ralph Cromwell
Sir William Crosse
Dafydd Llewwlyn
Sir 'Davy Gam'
Michael de la Pole
Edmund de la Pole
Sir John Devereux
Sir Thomas Dutton

PAGE 17
Sir William Eure [Evers]
Sir John Everingham
Sir Simon Felbrigge
Edmund Ferrers, Lord of Chartley
Sir Roger Fiennes
Henry Lord Fitz Hugh
Sir Thomas Fitzpayne
Sir Thomas Forster
Sir John Fortescue
Sir Walter Goldingham
Sir John Gresley
Sir Thomas Gresley

PAGE 18
Sir John Grey of Heton
Sir Richard Grey of Wilton
Sir William Harrington
Sir Richard Hastings
Sir Thomas Hawley
Sir John Heveningham
John Holland, Duke of Huntingdon
Sir John Hotham
Sir John Hoton
Sir Richard Huddleston
Sir Walter Hungerford
Sir Henry Hussey (Huse)

PAGE 19
Sir Richard Kighley
Sir Richard Lacon
Oliver Le Grose
Hamond Le Strange
Sir Philip Leche
Sir Roger Leche
Sir Peter Legh (Leigh) of Lyme
Sir William Legh (Leith) of Isell
Sir Roland Lenthall
Sir Alexander Loundes
Robert Lovell Esq
Sir Hugh Lowther

PAGE 20

John Lord Maltravers

Sir Nicholas Merbury

William Mering Esq.

Captain James Metcalfe

Thomas Montagu, Earl of Salisbury

Sir Nicholas Montgomery

Edmund Montimer, Earl of March

Sir Thomas Morley

Robert Morton Esq.

John Mowbray, Earl of Norfolk

Sir John Osbaldesten

John (ap Harry) Parry Esq.

PAGE 21

Nicholas Peche Esq.

John Pennington Esq.

Sir Henry Percy

Sir Thomas Percy

Sir William Phelip

Sir John Pilkington

Sir John Popham

Sir Stephen Popham

Sir William Porter

John Pympe Esq.

Sir Richard Radcliffe

Nicholas Radcliffe Esq.

PAGE 22

Richard Radcliffe Esq.

Sir Thomas Radcliffe of Derwentwater

Ralph Ramsey Esq.

Sir Thomas Rempston

Sir John Robessart

Sir Thomas Rokeby

John Lord Ros

Sir Robert Ros

John Rous of Baynton

Sir Thomas Routhe

Sir Walter 'Sandes' Sandys

Sir John Savage

PAGE 23

Sir Henry Scarisbrick

Sir William Scott

Richard Lord Scrope

Sir William Spayne

Sir Hugh Standish

Sir William Stanley of Hooton

Sir John Stanley

Sir Brian Stapleton

Sir Ralph Staveley

Sir Edward Stradling

Sir Thomas Strickland

Gilbert Lord Talbot

PAGE 24

Sir William Talbot

Sir Richard Tempest

Sir John Trelawny

Sir Roger Trumpington

Sir William Trussell

Baron James Tuchet

Sir Thomas Tunstall

Sir John Tyrell

William Tyrwhitt Esq.

Sir Gerard Ufflette

Sir Gilbert Umfraville

Robert Umfraville Esq.

PAGE 25

Robert Urswick Esq.

Roger Vaughan Esq of Bredwardine

Roger Vaughan Esq of Tretower

Richard de Vere, Earl of Oxford

Sir Richard Waldegrave

Sheriff Richard Waller

Sir John Waterton

Sir Thomas West

Robert Lord Willoughby

John Wodehouse Esq.

Richard Worthingtom Esq.

John Wyse Esq.

PAGE 26

Richard Woodville Esq.

William Gulby Esq

SirWilliam Lord Zouche

Sir Florence van Alkemade of Holland

King Henry

Edward Duke of York

Humphrey, Duke
of Gloucester

Thomas Lord Camoys

Sir Thomas Erpingham

Sir William Argentine

Sir Richard Arundel

Sir John Assheton

Sir Roger Aston

Sir Thomas Babington

Sir Robert Babthorpe

Sir John Baskerville

Sir John Beauchamp

Sir William Beauchamp

Sir Walter Beauchamp

Sir Charles Beaumont

John Bernard Esq.

Sir John Blount

Sir Ralph Bostock

William Lord Botreaux

Sir William Bouchier

John de Burgh

Sir John Calfe

14

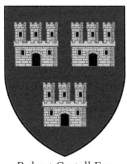

Robert Castell Esq.

Sir Thomas Charles

Sir Thomas Chaworth

John Cheney Esq.

William Chesterton Esq.

Sir John Chichester

John Lord Clifford

William Lord Clinton

Sir Hertong von Clux

Sir John Codringham

Sir John Cole

Sir John Croker

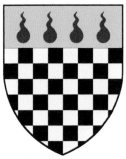

Sir John Colshill

Roger Corbet Esq.

Sir John Cornwall

Sir Edward Courtenay

Sir John Croker

Baron Ralph Cromwell

Sir William Crosse

Dafydd Llewwlyn
Sir 'Davy Gam'

Michael de la Pole

Edmund de la Pole

Sir John Devereux

Sir Thomas Dutton

Sir William Eure [Evers]

Sir John Everingham

Sir Simon Felbrigge

Edmund Ferrers
Lord of Chartley

Sir Roger Fiennes

Henry Lord Fitz Hugh

Sir Thomas Fitzpayne

Sir Thomas Forster

Sir John Fortescue

Sir Walter Goldingham

Sir john Gresley

Sir Thomas Gresley

17

Sir John Grey of Heton

Sir Richard Grey of Wilton

Sir William Harrington

Sir Richard Hastings

Sir Thomas Hawley

Sir John Heveningham

John Holland
Duke of Huntingdon

Sir John Hotham

Sir John Hoton

Sir Richard Huddleston

Sir Walter Hungerford

Sir Henry Hussey (Huse)

Sir Richard Kighley

Sir Richard Lacon

Oliver Le Grose

Hamond Le Strange

Sir Philip Leche

Sir Roger Leche

Sir Peter Legh (Leigh)
of Lyme

Sir William Legh (Leith)
of Isell

Sir Roland Lenthall

Sir Alexander Loundes

Robert Lovell Esq

Sir Hugh Lowther

19

John Lord Maltravers

Sir Nicholas Merbury

William Mering Esq.

Captain James Metcalfe

Thomas Montagu
Earl of Salisbury

Sir Nicholas Montgomery

Edmund Montimer
Earl of March

Sir Thomas Morley

Robert Morton Esq.

John Mowbray
Earl of Norfolk

Sir John Osbaldesten

John (ap Harry) Parry Esq.

Nicholas Peche Esq.

John Pennington Esq.

Sir Henry Percy

Sir Thomas Percy

Sir William Phelip

Sir John Pilkington

Sir John Popham

Sir Stephen Popham

Sir William Porter

John Pympe Esq.

Sir Richard Radcliffe

Nicholas Radcliffe Esq.

Richard Radcliffe Esq.

Sir Thomas Radcliffe
of Derwentwater

Ralph Ramsey Esq.

Sir Thomas Rempston

Sir John Robessart

Sir Thomas Rokeby

John Lord Ros

Sir Robert Ros

John Rous of Baynton

Sir Thomas Routhe

Sir Walter 'Sandes' Sandys

Sir John Savage

Sir Henry Scarisbrick

Sir William Scott

Richard Lord Scrope

Sir William Spayne

Sir Hugh Standish

Sir William Stanley
of Hooton

Sir John Stanley

Sir Brian Stapleton

Sir Ralph Staveley

Sir Edward Stradling

Sir Thomas Strickland

Gilbert Lord Talbot

Sir William Talbot

Sir Richard Tempest

Sir John Trelawny

Sir Roger Trumpington

Sir William Trussell

Baron James Tuchet

Sir Thomas Tunstall

Sir John Tyrell

William Tyrwhitt Esq.

Sir Gerard Ufflette

Sir Gilbert Umfraville

Robert Umfraville Esq.

Robert Urswick Esq.

Roger Vaughan Esq of
Bredwardine

Roger Vaughan Esq of
Tretower

Richard de Vere
Earl of Oxford

Sir Richard Waldegrave

Sheriff Richard Waller

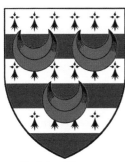

Sir John Waterton

Sir Thomas West

Robert Lord Willoughby

John Wodehouse Esq.

Richard Worthingtom Esq.

John Wyse Esq.

Richard Woodville Esq.   William Gulby Esq   William Lord Zouche

Sir Florence van Alkemade
of Holland

FRENCH COMBATANTS

THE COMMANDERS: PAGE 32

Charles d'Albret, Constable of France
Charles, Duke of Orléans
Jean, Duke of Bourbon & Auvergne
Jean Le Meingre Marshal Boucicaut
Edward, Duke of Bar
Jean 'Le Sage' Duke of Alençon

Philippe de Burgundy, Count of Nevers
Louis de Bourbon, Count of Vendome
Clignet de Brébant, Admiral of France
Antoine de Vergy, Count of Dammartin
Valeran de Raineval, Count of Fauquembergues

OTHER PERSONS OF DISTINCTION

PAGE 33

Baudouin d'Ailly Vidame of Amiens

Amedee d'Albon Lord of Baignols

Hugues d'Amboise Lord of Chaumont-Sur-Loire

Pierre d'Amiens Lord of Regnauville

Jean d'Angennes

Guillaume 'Oranglois' d'Anvin de Hardenthun

Jean Lord of Applaincourt

Dreux d'Argies Lord of Bethencourt

Maillard d'Assonville

Arnould d'Audregnies

Jean 'Hutin' Lord of Aumont

Hugues d'Auteux

PAGE 34

David, Lord of Auxy

Philippe d'Auxy Lord of Dompierre

Guillaume, Lord of Averholt

Renault, Lord of Azincourt

Waleran d'Azincourt

Jean de Bailleul

Jean de Bar Lord of Puisaye

Jean, Baron of Bauffremont

Antoine de Beauffort Lord of Avesnes

Colinet, Lord of Beauvais

Yvain de Beauval Lord of Ygnaucourt

Jean de Beauvoir Lord of Beauvoir-sur-Authie

PAGE 35

Pierre de Beauvoir Lord of Blancfosse

Hugues, Lord of Bellay

Bertrand de Bellay

Baudouin de Belleval

Pierre 'Baudrain' de Belloy

Jacques de Berlaymont Lord of Solre-le-Chateau

Adrien de Bernieulles

Colart de Bethune Lord of Berlettes

Jean 'Locres' de Bethune Lord of Autrches

Jean, Lord of Biez

Jean du Blaisel

Henry, Count of Blamont

PAGE 36

Bertrand de Blois

Jean de Blondel Baron of Longvilliers

Pierre de Blosset Lord of St Pierre-en-Caux

Jean du Bois Lord of Annequin

Charles de Boissey

Colinet, Lord of Boissey

Henri de Boissy Lord of Chaulnes

Robert de Bonnay Lord of Menetou

Jean, Lord of Bonneval

Aleaume, Lord of Boufflers

Louis de Bourbon Lord of Preaux

Antoine de Bourgogne Duke of Brabant

PAGE 37

Aleaume, Lord of Bournonville

Enguerrand 'Gamot'de Bournonville Lord of Chateaubricon

Bertrand 'Bastard' of Bournonville

Guillaume 'Witard' Lord of Bours

Louis, Lord of Bousies

Charles Boutery Viscount of Maisnieres

Gobert de la Bove Lord of Cilly

Pierre de Boylesve Lord of Forjan

Athis de Brimeu

Antoine, Lord of Brouilly

Attic de Brucamps

Jacques de la Brun Lord of Palaiseau

PAGE 38

Jean du Buat Lord of Brace

Jean, Lord of Bueil

Charles d'Artois Count of Eu

Jean de Cambout Lord of Vaurion

Colart, Count of Cambray

Jean, Lord of Caurroy

Jean 'le Stammerer' de Cayeu Lord of Vismes

Robert de Chabannes Lord of Chalus

Gallahaut de Chailly

Jean de Chalons Lord of Ligny-le-Chatel

Thibaut de Chantemerle

Hector de Chartres Lord of Ons-en-Bray

PAGE 39

Michel de Chasteler Lord of Moulbais

Guyon de Chateaubriand Lord of Roches

Jacques de Chateaugiron

Charles de Chatillon Lord of Survilliers

Hughes de Chatillon Lord of Leuze Blais

Jacques de Chatillon Lord of Dampierre

Robert de Chatillon Lord of Douy and Bry

Jean de Chaule Lord of Brétigny

Louis, Lord of Chepoy

George de Chesnel Lord of la Ballue

Guillaume de Chevenon Lord of Pacy

Gilles de Chin Lord of Same & Busigny

PAGE 40

Jean 'Lancelot' de Clary

Jean de Clere Baron of La Croix-St-Leufroy

Vigor de Clinchamps Lord of Meserets

Jean de Coetquen Marshal of Brittany

Arnaud de Corbie Lord of Auneuil

Lancelot de Coucy

Guillaume, Baron & Lord of Courcy

Baudouin 'Yvain' de Cramailles Lord of Saponay

Jean de Craon Lord of Chateaudun

Raoul 'l'Etendard' Lord of Crequy

Guillaume, Lord of Crevecoeur

Jean, Lord of Croy

PAGE 41

Jean II de Croy

Beraud I de Dauphin Lord of Saint-Esprit

Beraud II de Dauphin

Guichard de Dauphin Lord of Jaligny

Robert de Dauphin Lord of Chalus

Jean, Viscount of Domart

Gauvain de Dreux Vidame & Baron of d'Esneval

Jean de Dreux Lord of Houlbec

Baudouin Lord of Epagny

Guillaume d'Equennes Viscount of Poix

Alemand d'Escaussines (Flemish Knight)

Jean, Lord of Esclaibes

PAGE 42

Jean 'Le Baudrain' d'Esne Lord of Beauvoir

Charles d'Estouteville Lord of Blainville

Jean d'Estouteville

Jean, Senechal of Eu

Thiebaut du Fay Lord of Hiencourt

Jean de Fayel Viscount of Breteuil

Oliver, Lord of La Feillee

Raoul de Ferrieres

Mathieu 'Artistel' Lord of Fieffes

Aubert de Flamenc Lord of Canny

Raoul, Le Bastard of Flandres

Guillaume de la Folie

PAGE 43

Guillaume de Folin Lord of Dampierre

Jean, Lord of Folleville

Jean de Fontaines Lord of Neufville-au-Bois

Guillaume de la Forest

Guillaume de Fortescu

Jean de Fosseux Lord of Auteville

Walleran de Fougieres Lord of Fouqueroles

Jean 'Malarbe' Lord of Frechencourt

Robert 'Brunel' de Fretel Lord of Hubercourt

Jean de Fricamps Lord of La Riviere de Thibouville

Robert de Gamaches Lord of Chauvincourt

Aleaume, Lord of Gapennes

PAGE 44

Jean de Garancieres Captain of Caen

Jean du Gardin

Guillaume de Gaucourt Lord of Rouen

Henri de Gavre Lord of Rassenghem

Herve de Genevieres Captain of Crotoy Castle

Louis de Ghistelles (Flemish Knight)

Jean Giffard Lord of Plessis-Giffard

Pierre 'Moradas' Gougeul Lord of Rouville

Guy Goule Lord of Pande

Edward, Count de Grandpre

Jean de Gres

Roland 'de Bruges' van Gruuthuse

PAGE 45

Baugeois, Lord of Gribauval

Renaud de Gribauval

Hainaiut, Lord of Fagnolles

Jean de la Hamaide

Jean de Hamel Lord of Bellenglise

Robert, Lord of Hames

Caruel de Hangard

Jean, Lord of Hangest

Guerard d'Harcourt Baron of Bonnetable

Jacques d'Harcourt Baron of Montgommery

Jean VII, Count of Harcourt

Robert d'Harcourt Lord of Beaumenil

PAGE 46

Guillaume d'Harville Lord of Chaulandry des Bordes

Simon de Harvrech

Gerard, lord of Haucourt-en-Cambreis

Pierre de Haverskerque Lord of Rasse

Jacques, Lord of Heilly, Marshal of France

Robert de Hellande Lord of Lamberville

Jean de Henin

Lord of Henne

Michel, Lord of Hertaing

Jacques de Heu

Jacques de la Heuze Lord of Heuditot

Francis, Lord of Honschoote (Flemish Knight)

PAGE 47

Guillaume, Lord of Hornes

Jean de Humieres Lord of Bouzincourt

Gerard, Lord of Inchy

Guillaume de Ivry Baron of Ivry & Breval

Jean de Jeumont Lord & Baron of Barbançon

Thibaut, Lord of Lameth

Henri de la Lande

Guillebert de Lannoy Lord of Beaumont

Jean, Lord of Lannoy

Pierre 'Lamont' de Lannoy Lord of Obriscourt

Jacques de Lichtervelde Baron of Coolscamp

Philippe, Lord of Liedekerque

PAGE 48

Jean, Baron of Ligne

Jean, Lord of L'Ile-Bouchard

Jacques, Lord of Longroy

Guillaume, Lord of Longueil

Jean, Lord of Longueval

Ferry de Lorraine Count of Vaudemont

Jean de Lorris Lord of Beaurain

Jean de Lully

Pierre 'Pierron' de Lupe

Colart, Lord of Mailly

Jean d'Mailly Lord of Authieulles

Lionel de Maldeghem

PAGE 49

Jean de Malestroit Lord of Combourg

Jean de Malestroit Lord of Sales

Pierre de Mallet

Pierre, Lord of Mametz

Palamede de Marquais

Jean, Lord of Marquetes

Guillaume de Martel Lord of Bacqueville

Dreux de Mello Lord of Saint-Brice

Guillaume de Melun Count of Tancarville

Pierre de Mill

Jean de Monceau Lord of Tignonville

Simon de Monchaux

PAGE 50

Charles, Lord of Montagu

Bertrand de Montauban

Colart de Montbertaut

Jean, Lord of Montcavrel

Renaud de Montejan Lord of Gillebourg

Jean, Lord of Montenay

Tristan, Lord of Montholon

Robert, Lord of Montigny

Charles de Montigny-St-Christophe

Louis 'Beaussault' de Montmorency

Simon, Lord of Morainvilliers

Guillaume de Morin Lord of Loudon

PAGE 51

Yvon de Morvillers

Artus 'Goulart' Lord of Moy

Enguerrand de Nedonchel

Jean 'Baugeois' de Nedonchel Lord of Beuvriere

Guy de Nesle Lord of Offemont

Raoul de Nesle Lord of Saint-Crepin

Huges, Lord of Neufville

Topinet de la Neufville

Pierre 'The One-Eyed' de Noailles

Jean 'The White Knight' Lord of Noyelles

Jean, Lord of Occoches

Colart 'Estourdi' d'Ognies

PAGE 52

Pierre d'Orgemont Lord of Chavercy

Bertrand de Paynel Lord of Olondes

Philippe de Poitiers Lord of Arcy

Rogues de Poix Lord of Ignaucourt

Colart de la Porte Lord of Bellincourt

Lord of Potes

Heylard, Lord of Poucques

Girard de Poutraines Lord of Pontrohart

Jacques, Lord of Preaulx

Godefroy de Prouville

Guillaume de Prunele

Bridoul de Puisieux

PAGE 53

Quenoulles 'The Stammerer'

Jean, Lord of Quesnoy

Guy 'Boort' Quieret Lord of Heuchin

Huges 'Hutin' Quieret

George, Lord of Quievrain

Colart de la Rachie Lord of Belincourt

Jean de Raguenel Viscount of Belliere

Aubert de Raineval Lord of Bethencourt

David de Rambures Crossbow Master

Jean 'Lens' Lord of Recourt

Pierre 'The Carpentier' Lord of Remy

Foulques 'Galois'de Renty Lord of Embry

PAGE 54

Foulques d'Riboulle Lord of Asse

Arthur de Richemont Duke of Brittany

Perceval de Ricquebourg

Euguerrand de la Riviere Lord of Perchin

Guy, Lord of La Roche Guyon

Jean de Rochechouart Lord of Morlemart

Edward, Viscount of Rohan

Guillaume, Lord of Roncherolles

Robert, Lord of Ronnay

Pierre de Rosimbos

Jean de Roucy Count of Braine

Mathieu 'Borgne' de Rouvroy Lord of Saint-Simon

PAGE 55

Mathieu, Lord of Roye

Lancelot de Rubempre

Philippe de Runes Lord of Hacqueville

Le Bon de Sains

Laurent, Lord of Saint-Beuve

Pierre, Lord of Saint-Cler

Jean de Sainte-Maure Lord of Montgauger

Bertrand de Saint-Gilles

Godefroy de Saint-Marc

Raoul de Saint-Remy

Pons de Saluces Lord of
Chateauneuf

Guillaume, Lord of
Saveuse

PAGE 56

Charles de Savoisy Lord
of Seignelay

Lord of Schonvelde
(Flemish)

Colinet, Lord of Sempy

Jean de Soissons Lord of
Moreuil

Floridas de Souich

Charles de Soyécourt
Lord of Mouy

Pierre 'Sarrazin' Lord of
Tencques

Jean de Tilly Lord of
Chambois

Philippe de Wissocq Lord
of Gapennes

Agne de la Tour Lord of
Oliergues

Ponchon de la Tour

Pierre de Tourzel Lord
of
Alegre & Auvergne

PAGE 57

Jean de Tramecourt

Georges de La Tremoille
Count of Guines

Guillaume de Trie Lord
of Fontenay

Jean de Tyrel Lord of
Poix

Louis de Tyrel Lord of
Brimeu

Guillaume de Le Vayan
Captain of Jugon Castle

Jean la Veneur Lord of
Man & Saint-Elier

Jacques, Count of
Ventadour

Guillaume, Lord of Ver

Louis de Vertaing

Jean Le Vicomte Lord of
Tremlay

Jean 'Porus' de Viefville
Lord of Thiennes

PAGE 58

Yves, Lord of Vieuxpont

Pierre, Lord of Villaines

Jean de Waencourt Lord
of Pont-Remy

Alain de Wandonne

Gilles, Lord of Wargnies

Lord of Warluzel

Arnould de
Waudringhem

Gilles de Waudripont

Robert I, Lord of Wavrin

Robert II de Wavrin

Jean, Lord of Werchin

Robert de Wignacourt

Charles d'Albret
Constable of France

Charles, Duke of Orléans

Jean, Duke of Bourbon
& Auvergne

Jean Le Meingre
Marshal Boucicaut

Edward, Duke of Bar

Jean 'Le Sage'
Duke of Alençon

Philippe de Burgundy
Count of Nevers

Louis de Bourbon
Count of Vendome

Clignet de Brébant
Admiral of France

Antoine de Vergy
Count of Dammartin

Valeran de Raineval
Count of Fauquembergues

Baudouin d'Ailly
Vidame of Amiens

Amedee d'Albon
Lord of Baignols

Hugues d'Amboise, Lord of
Chaumont-Sur-Loire

Pierre d'Amiens
Lord of Regnauville

Jean d'Angennes

Guillaume 'Oranglois'
d'Anvin de Hardenthun

Jean, Lord of Applaincourt

Dreux d'Argies
Lord of Bethencourt

Maillard d'Assonville

Arnould d'Audregnies

Jean 'Hutin'
Lord of Aumont

Hugues d'Auteux

33

David, Lord of Auxy

Philippe d'Auxy
Lord of Dompierre

Guillaume,
Lord of Averholt

Renault, Lord of Azincourt

Waleran d'Azincourt

Jean de Bailleul

Jean de Bar
Lord of Puisaye

Jean, Baron
of Bauffremont

Antoine de Beauffort
Lord of Avesnes

Colinet, Lord of Beauvais

Yvain de Beauval
Lord of Ygnaucourt

Jean de Beauvoir, Lord of
Beauvoir-sur-Authie

Pierre de Beauvoir
Lord of Blancfosse

Hugues, Lord of Bellay

Bertrand de Bellay

Baudouin de Belleval

Pierre 'Baudrain' de Belloy

Jacques de Berlaymont
Lord of Solre-le-Chateau

Adrien de Bernieulles

Colart de Bethune
Lord of Berlettes

Jean 'Locres' de Bethune
Lord of Autrches

Jean, Lord of Biez

Jean du Blaisel

Henry, Count of Blamont

Bertrand de Blois

Jean de Blondel
Baron of Longvilliers

Pierre de Blosset
Lord of St Pierre-en-

Jean du Bois
Lord of Annequin

Charles de Boissey

Colinet, Lord of Boissey

Henri de Boissy
Lord of Chaulnes

Robert de Bonnay
Lord of Menetou

Jean, Lord of Bonneval

Aleaume, Lord of Boufflers

Louis de Bourbon
Lord of Preaux

Antoine de Bourgogne
Duke of Brabant

Aleaume, Lord of
Bournonville

Enguerrand 'Gamot'de
Bournonville,

Bertrand 'Bastard' of
Bournonville

Guillaume 'Witard'
Lord of Bours

Louis, Lord of Bousies

Charles Boutery
Viscount of Maisnieres

Gobert de la Bove
Lord of Cilly

Pierre de Boylesve
Lord of Forjan

Athis de Brimeu

Antoine, Lord of Brouilly

Attic de Brucamps

Jacques de la Brun
Lord of Palaiseau

Jean du Buat
Lord of Brace

Jean, Lord of Bueil

Charles d'Artois
Count of Eu

Jean de Cambout
Lord of Vaurion

Colart, Count of Cambray

Jean, Lord of Caurroy

Jean 'Le Stammerer' de
Cayeu, Lord of Vismes

Robert de Chabannes
Lord of Chalus

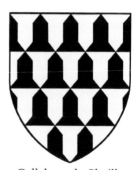

Gallahaut de Chailly

Jean de Chalons
Lord of Ligny-le-Chatel

Thibaut de Chantemerle

Hector de Chartres
Lord of Ons-en-Bray

Michel de Chasteler
Lord of Moulbais

Guyon de Chateaubriand
Lord of Roches

Jacques de Chateaugiron

Charles de Chatillon
Lord of Survilliers

Hughes de Chatillon
Lord of Leuze Blais

Jacques de Chatillon
Lord of Dampierre

Robert de Chatillon
Lord of Douy and

Jean de Chaule
Lord of Brétigny

Louis, Lord of Chepoy

George de Chesnel
Lord of la Ballue

Guillaume de Chevenon
Lord of Pacy.

Gilles de Chin
Lord of Same & Busigny

39

Jean 'Lancelot' de Clary

Jean de Clere Baron of La Croix-St-Leufroy

Vigor de Clinchamps Lord of Meserets

Jean de Coetquen Marshal of Brittany

Arnaud de Corbie Lord of Auneuil

Lancelot de Coucy

Guillaume, Baron & Lord of Courcy

Baudouin 'Yvain' de Cramailles, Lord of Saponay

Jean de Craon Lord of Chateaudun

Raoul 'l'Etendard' Lord of Crequy

Guillaume, Lord of Crevecoeur

Jean, Lord of Croy

40

Jean II de Croy

Beraud I de Dauphin
Lord of Saint-Esprit

Beraud II de Dauphin

Guichard de Dauphin
Lord of Jaligny

Robert de Dauphin
Lord of Chalus

Jean, Viscount of Domart

Gauvain de Dreux, Vidame
& Baron of d'Esneval

Jean de Dreux
Lord of Houlbec

Baudouin, Lord of Epagny

Guillaume d'Equennes
Viscount of Poix

Alemand d'Escaussines
(Flemish Knight)

Jean, Lord of Esclaibes

Jean 'Le Baudrain' d'Esne
Lord of Beauvoir

Charles d'Estouteville
Lord of Blainville

Jean d'Estouteville

Jean, Senechal of Eu

Thiebaut du Fay
Lord of Hiencourt

Jean de Fayel
Viscount of Breteuil

Oliver, Lord of La Feillee

Raoul de Ferrieres

Mathieu 'Artistel'
Lord of Fieffes

Aubert de Flamenc
Lord of Canny

Raoul, Le Bastard of
Flandres

Guillaume de la Folie

Guillaume de Folin
Lord of Dampierre

Jean, Lord of Folleville

Jean de Fontaines
Lord of Neufville-au-Bois

Guillaume de La Forest

Guillaume de Fortescu

Jean de Fosseux
Lord of Auteville

Walleran de Fougieres
Lord of Fouqueroles

Jean 'Malarbe'
Lord of Frechencourt

Robert 'Brunel' de Fretel
Lord of Hubercourt

Jean de Fricamps, Lord of
La Riviere de Thibouville

Robert de Gamaches
Lord of Chauvincourt

Aleaume, Lord of Gapennes

43

Jean de Garancieres
Captain of Caen

Jean du Gardin

Guillaume de Gaucourt
Lord of Rouen

Henri de Gavre
Lord of Rassenghem

Herve de Genevieres
Captain of Crotoy Castle

Louis de Ghistelles
(Flemish Knight)

Jean Giffard
Lord of Plessis-Giffard

Pierre 'Moradas' Gougeul
Lord of Rouville

Guy Goule,
Lord of Pande

Edward,
Count de Grandpre

Jean de Gres

Roland 'de Bruges' van
Gruuthuse

Baugeois
Lord of Gribauval

Renaud de Gribauval

Hainaiut,
Lord of Fagnolles

Jean de la Hamaide

Jean de Hamel
Lord of Bellenglise

Robert, Lord of Hames

Caruel de Hangard

Jean, Lord of Hangest

Guerard d'Harcourt
Baron of Bonnetable

Jacques d'Harcourt
Baron of Montgommery

Jean VII
Count of Harcourt

Robert d'Harcourt
Lord of Beaumenil

45

Guillaume d'Harville, Lord
of Chaulandry des Bordes

Simon de Harvrech

Gerard, Lord of
Haucourt-en-Cambreis

Pierre de Haverskerque
Lord of Rasse

Jacques, Lord of Heilly,
Marshal of France

Robert de Hellande
Lord of Lamberville

Jean de Henin

Lord of Henne

Michel, Lord of Hertaing

Jacques de Heu

Jacques de la Heuze
Lord of Heuditot

Francis, Lord of Honschoote
(Flemish Knight)

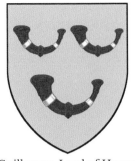

Guillaume, Lord of Hornes

Jean de Humieres
Lord of Bouzincourt

Gerard, Lord of Inchy

Guillaume de Ivry
Baron of Ivry & Breval

Jean de Jeumont, Lord &
Baron of Barbançon

Thibaut, Lord of Lameth

Henri de la Lande

Guillebert de Lannoy
Lord of Beaumont

Jean, Lord of Lannoy

Pierre 'Lamont' de Lannoy
Lord of Obriscourt

Jacques de Lichtervelde
Baron of Coolscamp

Philippe, Lord of
Liedekerque

47

Jean, Baron of Ligne

Jean, Lord of
L'Ile-Bouchard

Jacques,
Lord of Longroy

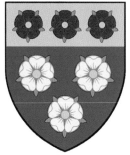

Guillaume,
Lord of Longueil

Jean, Lord of Longueval

Ferry de Lorraine
Count of Vaudemont

Jean de Lorris
Lord of Beaurain

Jean de Lully

Pierre 'Pierron' de Lupe

Colart, Lord of Mailly

Jean d'Mailly
Lord of Authieulles

Lionel de Maldeghem

Jean de Malestroit
Lord of Combourg

Jean de Malestroit
Lord of Sales

Pierre de Mallet

Pierre, Lord of Mametz

Palamede de Marquais

Jean, Lord of Marquetes

Guillaume de Martel
Lord of Bacqueville

Dreux de Mello
Lord of Saint-Brice

Guillaume de Melun
Count of Tancarville

Pierre de Mill

Jean de Monceau
Lord of Tignonville

Simon de Monchaux

Charles, Lord of Montagu

Bertrand de Montauban

Colart de Montbertaut

Jean, Lord of Montcavrel

Renaud de Montejan
Lord of Gillebourg

Jean, Lord of Montenay

Tristan,
Lord of Montholon

Robert, Lord of Montigny

Charles de
Montigny-St-Christophe

Louis 'Beaussault' de
Montmorency

Simon, Lord of
Morainvilliers

Guillaume de Morin
Lord of Loudon

50

Yvon de Morvillers

Artus 'Goulart'
Lord of Moy

Enguerrand de Nedonchel

Jean 'Baugeois' de Nedonchel
Lord of Beuvriere

Guy de Nesle
Lord of Offemont

Raoul de Nesle
Lord of Saint-Crepin

Huges, Lord of Neufville

Topinet de la Neufville

Pierre 'The One-Eyed'
de Noailles

Jean 'The White Knight'
Lord of Noyelles

Jean, Lord of Occoches

Colart 'Estourdi' d'Ognies

51

Pierre d'Orgemont
Lord of Chavercy

Bertrand de Paynel
Lord of Olondes

Philippe de Poitiers
Lord of Arcy

Rogues de Poix
Lord of Ignaucourt

Colart de la Porte
Lord of Bellincourt

Lord of Potes

Heylard, Lord of Poucques

Girard de Poutraines
Lord of Pontrohart

Jacques, Lord of Preaulx

Godefroy de Prouville

Guillaume de Prunele

Bridoul de Puisieux

Quenoulles
'The Stammerer'

Jean, Lord of Quesnoy

Guy 'Boort' Quieret
Lord of Heuchin

Hughes 'Hutin' Quieret

George, Lord of Quievrain

Colart de la Rachie
Lord of Belincourt

Jean de Raguenel
Viscount of Belliere

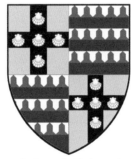

Aubert de Raineval
Lord of Bethencourt

David de Rambures
Crossbow Master

Jean 'Lens'
Lord of Recourt

Pierre 'The Carpentier'
Lord of Remy

Foulques 'Galois'de Renty
Lord of Embry

Foulques d'Riboulle
Lord of Asse

Arthur de Richemont
Duke of Brittany

Perceval de Ricquebourg

Euguerrand de la Riviere
Lord of Perchin

Guy, Lord of La Roche
Guyon

Jean de Rochechouart
Lord of Morlemart

Edward, Viscount of Rohan

Guillaume, Lord of
Roncherolles

Robert, Lord of Ronnay

Pierre de Rosimbos

Jean de Roucy
Count of Braine

Mathieu 'Borgne' de Rouvroy
Lord of Saint-Simon

54

Mathieu, Lord of

Lancelot de Rubempre

Philippe de Runes
Lord of Hacqueville

Le Bon de Sains

Laurent
Lord of Saint-Beuve

Pierre, Lord of Saint-

Jean de Sainte-Maure
Lord of Montgauger

Bertrand de Saint-Gilles

Godefroy de Saint-Marc

Raoul de Saint-Remy

Pons de Saluces
Lord of Chateauneuf

Guillaume
Lord of Saveuse

Charles de Savoisy
Lord of Seignelay

Lord of Schonvelde
(Flemish)

Colinet, Lord of Sempy

Jean de Soissons
Lord of Moreuil

Floridas de Souich

Charles de Soyécourt
Lord of Mouy

Pierre 'Sarrazin'
Lord of Tencques

Jean de Tilly
Lord of Chambois

Philippe de Wissocq
Lord of Gapennes

Agne de la Tour
Lord of Oliergues

Ponchon de la Tour

Pierre de Tourzel Lord of
Alegre & Auvergne

Jean de Tramecourt

Georges de La Tremoille
Count of Guines

Guillaume de Trie
Lord of Fontenay

Jean de Tyrel
Lord of Poix

Louis de Tyrel
Lord of Brimeu

Guillaume de Le Vayan
Captain of Jugon Castle

Jean la Veneur
Lord of Man & Saint-Elier

Jacques, Count of
Ventadour

Guillaume, Lord of Ver

Louis de Vertaing

Jean Le Vicomte
Lord of Tremlay

Jean 'Porus' de Viefville
Lord of Thiennes

Yves, Lord of Vieuxpont

Pierre, Lord of Villaines

Jean de Waencourt
Lord of Pont-Remy

Alain de Wandonne

Gilles, Lord of Wargnies

Lord of Warluzel

Arnould de Waudringhem

Gilles de Waudripont

Robert I, Lord of Wavrin

Robert II de Wavrin

Jean, Lord of Werchin

Robert de Wignacourt

MORE FRENCH NAMES

The following names are knights and other dignitaries that the author could not be sure of the coat of arms or marks of cadency.

Bearing in mind that all these French names in this book are mostly from lists of figures either killed or taken prisoner, it is sad how many French families must have been decimated by the result of this battle.

Eustache, Lord of Ambrines

Antoine d'Ambrines (son of above)

Jacques d'Applaincourt (son of Jean)

Jean d'Archeries

Robert de Bar, Lord of Oisy

Briffaut de Berlaymont (brother of Jacques)

Charles Blondel (son of Jean)

Jacques de Brussy

Bertrand de Buisson

Guillaume de Caurroy (brother of Jean)

Mathieu 'Payen' de Cayeu (brother of Jean)

Pierre de Chartres (brother of Hector)

Jean de Chartres (brother of Hector)

Fastre de Chasteler (brother of Michel)

Gaspard de Chatillon (brother of Hughes)

Simon de Craon, Lord of Clacy

Antoine de Craon, Lord of Beauverger

Amaury de Craon, Lord of Briolay

Jean de Crequy, Lord of Molliens

Archambaut de Croy (son of Jean I)

Nicholas 'Colart' d'Estouteville, Lord of Torcy

Enguerran de Fieffes

Colart de Fiennes, Captain of Castle Pierrefonds

Enguerran de Fontaines (son of Jean)

Charles de Fontaines (son of Jean)

Colart de Fosseux (son of Jean)

Lancelot de Fromessant

Guillaume de Gamaches

Jean de Gourle, Lord of Wiameville

Gilbert de Gribauval (brother of Baugeois)

Gerard de Herbaumes, Captain of Castle Coucy

Mathieu de Humieres (son of Jean)

Dreux de Humieres

Charles de Ivry (son of Guillaume)

Guillaume de la Haye

Philippe de la Roche Guyon (brother of Guy)

Jacques de l'Eschelle

Hughes de Lannoy, Lord of Santes

Michel de Ligne, Lord of Barbancon

Raoul de Longueil (son of Guillaume)

Alain de Longueval, Lord of Franconville

Griffon de Lully (brother of Jean)

Philippe de Maldeghem (brother of Lionel)

Geoffroy de Malestroit

Lancelot de Mametz (brother of Pierre)

Raoul de Mametz

Aubert de Marbres

Jean Martel (son of Guillaume)

Floridas de Moreuil

Tristan de Moy (brother of Artus)

Gamart de Nedonchel (brother of Jean)

Baudouin de Noyelles (brother of Jean)

Bertrand d'Ongnies (brother of Colart)

Dreux d'Ongnies (brother of Colart)

Pierre de Quieret (brother of Guy & Hughes)

Henri de Quievrain (brother of George)

Jean de Rambures (brother of David)

Hughes de Rambures (brother of David)

Philippe de Rambures (brother of David)

Colart de Rasse

Gerard I de Recourt (son of Gerard II)

Jean 'Castelet' de Renty

Philippe de la Roche Guyon (brother of Guy)

Jean, Lord of Ront

Leonnet de Ruys

Guillaume 'Galois' Rouvroy (brother of Mathieu)

Hector de Saveuses (brother of Guillaume)

Philippe de Saveuses (brother of Guillaume)

Jean de Sempy

Gilles de Soyecourt (son of Charles)

Renaud de Tramecourt (brother of Jean)

Jacques de Trie (same family as Guillaume de Trie)

Jeanet Tyrel de Poix (son of Jean Tyrel)

Charles de Ventadour

Charles de Villaines (brother of Pierre)

Guillaume de Villers, Lord of Verderonne)

Renaut de Villers (same family as above)

Robinet de Waencourt

Martelet du Walhoun

Try as they might the French could find no way through the English line. (Illustration by Henry J Ford)

NOTES

NOTES

NOTES

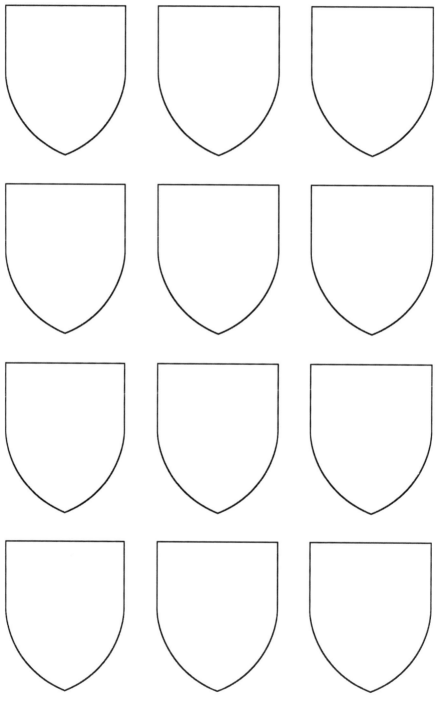